Other Press · New York

The Return
of the
Blue Cat

OTHER BOOKS BY F. D. REEVE

POETRY
In the Silent Stones
The Blue Cat
Nightway
Concrete Music
The Moon and Other Failures
The Urban Stampede and Other Poems
A World You Haven't Seen

FICTION
The Red Machines
Just Over the Border
The Brother
White Colors
A Few Rounds of Old Maid & Other Stories

CRITICISM
Aleksandr Blok: Between Image and Idea
Robert Frost in Russia
The Russian Novel
The White Monk: An Essay on Dostoevsky and Melville

TRANSLATIONS
Five Short Novels by Turgenev
Nineteenth Century Russian Plays (The Norton Library)
Twentieth Century Russian Plays
Contemporary Russian Drama
The Nobel Lecture by Alexander Solzhenitsyn
The Garden by Bella Akhmadulina

EDITED COLLECTIONS
After the Storm: Poems on the Persian Gulf War (*with Jay Meek*)
Winged Spirits (Collages by Zaleski and 24 Contemporary Poems)

The Return of the Blue Cat

Poems by F. D. Reeve

Other Press · New York

Earlier versions of some of these poems previously appeared in *The Blue Cat*, New York: Farrar, Straus & Giroux, 1972; others have recently been in *The American Poetry Review*, *The Antioch Review*, *Pivot*, and *The Sewanee Review*, whose editors are gratefully acknowledged.

Special thanks to Ellen Vanook, Stacy Hague and Mira S. Park for their hidden roles in making this book.

Photos, pages 81–86, © 2005 Sean Sime

Production Editor: Mira S. Park
Book design by Natalya Balnova

This book was set in 10.5 pt ITC Officina Sans LT by Alpha Graphics of Pittsfield, New Hampshire.

10 9 8 7 6 5 4 3 2 1

Library of Congress Cataloging-in-Publication Data
Reeve, F. D. (Franklin D.), 1928-
The return of the blue cat / by F.D. Reeve.
    p. cm.
ISBN 1-59051-172-7 (pbk. : alk. paper) 1. Cats—Poetry. I. Title.
PS3568.E44R48 2005
811'.54—dc22

2004018801

For Joan J *and* Edward A

Some, that are mad if they behold a cat,
. . . a harmless, necessary cat.

—The Merchant of Venice

CONTENTS

PREFACE

Cat—the word fades in the mists of history. Ever since the oceans receded and left a spit of dry land, *felix domesticus*, like the elegant black statue with the delicately arched back, the short ears and long forelegs bearing forever the self-possessed nobility of ancient Egypt, has prowled the dark and helped patron goddess Bastet protect us. An avuncular lion in painted limestone came out of the desert; a thousand years later, an alabaster cat with rock crystal and copper eyes held cosmetics for a lovely lady to prepare her face; and under the Ptolemies, while Alexander was conquering the Near East and Rome was taking over the Italian peninsula, the once-statuesque dark basalt cat—now a *felicia*—rounded her shoulders and pierced her ears with gold rings. In the Victorian period, while retaining her inner fire, she dressed herself out as a gray-spotted, white china doll with a bell collared to her neck.

Against all such tamings—including Pound's "Tame Cat" ("The purring of the invisible antennae / Is both stimulating and delightful")—came the Cat that Walked by Himself, the imaginative ordinator of all cats before and since. Born of Kipling's impulse to make up for his "best beloved" children narrative reasons for the animals' differences, the Cat appeared in one of the last stories told to Elsie and John after the tragic death of Josephine, who had demanded that the early stories be repeated exactly, "just so." In the story, Man and Woman live in a very nice Cave and cook their food over a fire. That draws Wild Dog, whom they domesticate. The Cat checks the place out, calls Dog's bargain "foolish," and returns to the Wet Wild Woods. Man and Woman then halter Horse, milk Cow and bear Baby, whereupon the Cat, who is "not a friend" and "not a servant," tricks Woman into an agreement, outwits her, and ends in Baby's arms after lapping milk by the warm fire until

Man and Dog return. He promises to catch mice so that not all men will throw things at him, and he stands ready to dart up a tree, though not all dogs will chase him, but whenever he wishes, he'll take off, for he is "the Cat that Walks by Himself" and all places are alike to him.

Kipling illustrated the *Just So Stories*, most famously portraying a strong, bandy-legged, saucy, moustachioed mouser with a full, brushy, handsome stern twitching high in the air as he heads down an avenue between two rows of black-limbed winter trees:

> This is the picture of the Cat that Walked by Himself, walking by his wild lone through the Wet Wild Woods and waving his wild tail. There is nothing else in the picture except some toadstools. They had to grow there because the woods were so wet.

Of course the Cat is walking *away*, and of course his back is straight and his tail is full and curving, and his gait is slightly angled, moderately swaggering, self-reliant and self-controlled. The Cat is porter of his own free will. Of all the domesticated animals only he came on his own terms, always reserving the right to run out from under anyone's dependence on him and his on anyone. You can do nothing about it: you can train a dog, harness a horse, tether a cow, but you can't even argue with a cat. He retains his dignity by asserting his free will. No matter where he is, he reserves his space.

Some thirty years ago the Blue Cat came out of thin air, not like the Cheshire Cat with a gigantic grin but like a lovely statuette animating itself after years of patiently watching the people's parade—rather as if waking from a long sleep, stretching, looking round, and saying, "For years you treated me as a projection of your secret selves; now that we're facing each other eye to eye, let me tell you what you look like." Before doing that, though, he talked a little about himself, got into a scrape or two, behaved in a strong-minded, strong-armed way and then apocalyptically vanished into the music of the spheres. I remembered him at the Polka Dot in White River Junction, and the rumble we had over what was his territory and what was mine, and I knew he had more lives coming—presumably eight at least—

but I had no way of knowing that our paths would cross again. One afternoon a while back, when I pulled off the highway to the Silver Diner—a cross between an old trolley and a Forties' train—there he was watching the door, waiting for his hash browns and Salisbury steak. He hung around in the city far longer than usual, coming and going at all times of the day, before disappearing again—this time, I think, on behalf of the people he believes in. He's not a singing cat or a musical cat, but he's a book-loving cat who tries to keep up with the latest and does slightly unusual things, like on days when kittens are jumping and batting at flies, he'll just for the hell of it thumb through a dictionary. I think he likes the thump of his paw and the sound of the pages turning.

His coming back was a surprise. When cats leave, as I said, you've no idea if they'll return. They behave the way you often wish you could. So, although I dared not count on seeing him again, I hoped I would. I suppose you'll point out that, since he has gone again, I'm back in the same boat? Not really, because this time we had what my grandmother called an especially good visit. I have a pretty good hunch why he came back.

First of all, he's a thoroughly smart American. In *The Devil's Dictionary*, Ambroise Bierce described one of the Blue Cat's generic ancestors from an ordinary citizen's point of view:

CAT, *n.*
 A soft, indestructible automaton provided by nature to be kicked when things go wrong in the domestic circle.

He knows that happens, but that's not how he sees himself. If you want to see him in his natural habitat, so to speak—if you happen to drop by the Silver Diner—or simply the next time you stop at a Blue Diamond—look for the Blue Cat breakfasting by himself, a little taller, a little leaner, a little handsomer than average, amiable, respectful of friends but almost always traveling alone. His shirtsleeves are tucked up; he wears jeans and a leather vest. He gets two little paper cups of applesauce with his pork chop, nods "thanks" for a second cup of coffee. Breasty young servers flirt with him; he listens to older ones' stories. His pickup is outside; it's cleaner, plainer, a little older than most.

When he first started driving the highways, he told the boys in the bar one day, he had an old White. But big changes were going on all around him—more highways, more malls, more pressure on him as a driver—until he said to himself, "Behind the wheel's no place for a cat." Oh, he liked the travel part, all right, but he decided he could do more as an organizer. So, he started traveling the country, talking with the locals, the shop stewards, setting up one arrangement after another. Nobody ever knew where he'd be next.

Personally, he's slim but muscular, well-trimmed, uncomplicated. He tidies up after every meal, washes regularly, and pays little attention to long-haired howlers or fluffy neckers. He prefers plainspokenness to verbal affectation and self-doubt to self-assertiveness. Some days he knows very well who he is; other days he fears he's a failure. He respects an individual's right to go hunting but distrusts all forms of militarism. Although he remains severely skeptical of social behavior (kings and policemen seeming to him ubiquitously tyrannical), if you ask him for a theory of social change, he'll smile condescendingly and walk away. I think he pities our ignorance; I know he abjures our obstinacy and stupidity. He prefers the poor to the rich on the grounds that, having less, they cheat less. He has done drugs. He holds no grudges. Once upon a time he organized his district and almost took over the city, but he, who was a fine fighter and an inspiring idealist, was no administrator: before he could twitch his tail, competitors had snatched his office from him. He likes sex and keeps trying to get off the street, especially since one of his daughters died there—but even though he's now well into the third—or maybe it's the fourth or even fifth—of his nine lives, he still can't. He respects his father but life after life does all he can to differentiate himself. The biggest change in him over the last thirty years is his coming to understand the pervasiveness of the corruption involved in political power and the importance of standing up against it.

He has long known that to do good you have to be able to do something useful well. He admires artistic skill no less than scientific invention, but he's certain that skill can't stand without meaning. "So, the trick is to find for each work the form that expresses the original experience's significance?"

I ask him. "The beautiful is moral," he says, pointing to the old engraving hanging on the wall left of the bar, "so, even wrecked, the Parthenon is the West's most perfectly proportioned building." He admits he doesn't know what Truth is ("If you want to know what Truth is, go to the soup societies") but he has a fair idea of what it isn't. He urges all young cats to do their best anyway.

From what he's said and done, I judge he's a courteous, outspoken, well-read, somewhat randy anarchist ready again to lay down one of his lives for what he believes. You can't ask for more.

THE COMEBACK CAT

Night is

        a dirty mountain

        flowers drifting on a windless ocean

        wild horses stampeding across a road

        a broken face

Over the earth's head

  its hot coals burning the sky

    a blue cat

        sails

        out of the sunrise

1

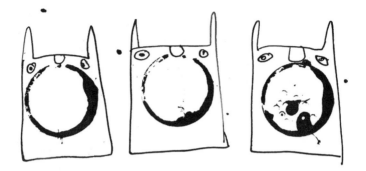

THE BLUE CAT AT THE LAUNDROMAT

Automatic washing machines:
Please remove all your clothes when the light goes out

—sign in a Boston laundromat

No matter where he nabs a bite,
in alley or saloon,
a cat will pause to clean his puss
and wash his pantaloons.

Well-dressed cats will always choose
to match partners with their clothes,

but the Blue Cat dancing cheek to cheek
  picks his true-love by the nose.

"A fig, my friends, for feline refinement
  when the light goes out.
Ladies and gents, buck naked spin round
  in the Washeteria Rout!"

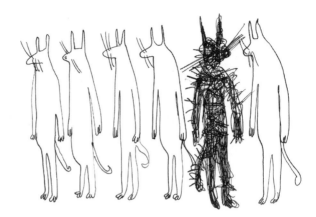

IDENTITY CRISIS

He was urged to prepare for success: "You never can tell,"
 he was told over and over; "others have made it;
  one dare not presume to predict. You never can tell.

Who's Who in America lists the order of cats
 in hunting, fishing, bird-watching, farming,
  domestic service—the dictionary order of cats

who have made it. Those not in the book are beyond the pale.
 Not to succeed in your chosen profession is unthinkable.
  Either you make it or—you're beyond the pale.

Do you understand?"

                    "No," he shakes his head.

    "Are you ready to forage for freedom?"

                              "No," he adds,

    "I mean, why is a cat always shaking his head?

Because he's thinking: who am I? I am not
    only one-ninth of myself. I always am
    all of the selves I have been and will be but am not."

"The normal cat," I tell him, "soon adjusts
    to others and to changing circumstances;
    he makes his way the way he soon adjusts."

"I can't," he says, "perhaps because I'm blue,
    big-footed, lop-eared, socially awkward, impotent,
    and I drink too much, whether because I'm blue

or because I like it, who knows. I want to escape
    at five o'clock into an untouchable world
where the top is the bottom and everyone wants to escape

from the middle, everyone, every day. I mean,
　　I have visions of two green eyes rising
　　out of the ocean, blinking, knowing what I mean."

"Never mind the picture, repeat after me
　　the Self's creed. What he tells you you
　　tells me and I repeats. Now, after me:

I love myself, I wish I would live well.
　　Your gift of love breaks through my self-defeat.
　　All prizes are blue. No cat admits defeat.
The next time that he lives he will live well."

THE BLUE CAT STUDIES HISTORY'S LESSONS

The Third Crusade

Six thousand rode out
      six thousand for war
      Philip and Frederick and Richard the First
      three cats and three armies
         crusading for Christ versus Saracen
            two drummers were drumming
            two manx thumping Heaven

Frederick drowned on the way
      the Germans went home

and Philip Augustus began to dream
of scaling white Dover
    instead of the tents of Jerusalem
        two witches were crooning
        two toms piping Heaven

Star hero at home
    blind fool in the field
    Richard wasted all his pride's wealth,
    enticed his descendants
        to keep plotting the wreck of Jerusalem
        two whorehounds were dancing
        two scumbags in Heaven

The patient the wise
    cool cat Saladin
    tamed the invaders brought shepherds
    and peace to the remnants
        of manger and mosque in Jerusalem
        two women still pray there

black-haired Rachel who honored
Jacob forever
and the slave Anis al-Jalis
who saved Nur al-Din

The French Revolution

On the other side of a wall
a tall
blue cat
in a pepper-and-salt tweed hat
is singing a roundelay:
Serpent plombé, tain de miroir,
enchanté de vous revoir.

A boy with a gun in hand
takes a stand
too late
at the open city gate

and has nothing to say:
> Instead, the cat: *Whoever you are,*
> *enchanté de vous revoir.*

A girl with a pen and rule
from school
pauses
to teach the cat the causes
of NO PARKING signs today:
> The cat: *O folle de désespoir,*
> *enchanté de vous revoir.*

A porcelain soldier shoots
and loots
the boy
and girl's plastic toy
world. The cat prays:
> *Seigneur, vite! Embrasse ce soir*
> *les âmes en peine qui veulent Te voir.*

The Great Wall is a screen
between
the sea
and all Arabia.
It lurks in memory,
which through the cat will say:
> *Ce n'est pas la mer à boire;*
> *enchanté de vous revoir.*

EARLY MORNING IN WHITE RIVER JUNCTION

Reality muddles together:
>   the phalanxes Ares has charge of
>   surrender to Aphrodite's
>   electric pomology whether
> led on by the sword or the nightie.

Felinity twitches a whisker.
>   Coherence applies for addresses.
>   A blasphemy opens the window
>   to let in Don Juan: cats know where
> their lady is quickly undressing.

A breakfast assignment is special
    if held in the Polka Dot Restaurant.
    Marie is the waitress, and Doris,
    the cook. Bright red mice dance around on
the walls. The hot jukebox tomorrows

the tune of a lay—oh, the piece now
    is grossly inflated. Havana
    cigars lie unwanted. A woman
    of parts expects to be totalled,
not beat with a Polish banana.

The cat that is blue tips his hat, true,
    and Anna smiles back from the register.
    They make up a pastry of tasteless
    boohoos with a dough once homogeneous.
Bacteria leaven their love. You

whose twenty pink eyes burn the darkness,
    start kissing your floozy and cursing,

but curtains, I say, to your restaurant
where love is a whistle or notice,
a pass at the slip of the solstice

northeast in the frozen direction
of Iceland. No, here a cat's hopping
shorts the glass fuse: "Next Selection"
remains in the rack, needle poised, while
out back in the bathroom a couple
are ripping it off without stopping.

Yes, here in the Polka Dot Restaurant
the pancakes and syrup are sweeter
than Gilead balm, and the promise
of finding a cat you can count on
is more than just reading the comics.

THE BLUE CAT & THE PARROT:
A Colloquy on a Summer Street Corner

A PARROT   Mark my words.
                  A penny for the homeless.
                  Mind the gap.

BLUE CAT   Perched on your post, you're silhouetted
                  like a sleepy cormorant against the moon.

PARROT   Shag me a fag.
                  I have an existential hunger
                  that like a V-8 drives my gab.

BLUE CAT   *No me fío de tú.*

PARROT   That's the lingo; use my phone;
when you reach God, you'll know who's home.

BLUE CAT   If the bear hadn't wanted a beer
he wouldn't have gone into the bar.
Which is better, black or red?

PARROT   Honest birds opt for Old Crow.
Never swim when you can row.
Don't trust the Reds or those who say
one if by Wall, two by Broadway.

BLUE CAT   Long-lived citizen, wit in disguise,
green gabber of grift, uncollared mark,
two bucks a try, three tries for a fin,
watch these shells, which one's it in?
Tell me where the little ball lies.

PARROT   East of the Sun, west of the Moon.
            A penny for the homeless.
            Mind the gap.

BLUE CAT   Hope like feathers blowing down a street
            rises from each formal opera house;
            you who cling to the sky with your feet
            confess you're overdressed for Heaven.

PARROT   These stoolie's clothes? A Moroccan *ghazze*
            sewed this gilded vest for me;
            but you, I see by your furry rump,
            are as bare-assed as a camel's hump.

BLUE CAT   Can you with no paws gather more than I?
            Canst climb a tree? Canst catch a fish?
            Canst lick blood gravy from a dish?
            How can you sing sweeter than I
            when you haven't even one open eye?
            Tell me, who's behind your back?

18

PARROT   My skeptical askance
and telepathic sense
name things three times more right
than simple chance.

BLUE CAT   Do you, like skunks, suck eggs in the dark?
Dare you attend rats' carnivals in Central Park?
Wouldn't your zoological friends think "hazmat"
to see a bird communicating with a cat?

PARROT   From where I sit
I will admit
the whole parade's ridiculous;
so why should you
feel what you do
is particularly conspicuous?
Eso occure siempre entre amigos.
Mind the gap.

BLUE CAT   There is no limit
             to the reasons one may hate another;
             all reasons are infinite.

PARROT   I can't see what you think
             but when you open your mouth
             your tongue is pink.

BLUE CAT   Of my comrades some survive
             dedicated to peaceful works;
             others paradoxically fight on
             across the seas or in the desert.

PARROT   Mark my words.

BLUE CAT   Count me out.

PARROT   A penny for the homeless.

BLUE CAT   Fines doubled in work areas.

PARROT   Mind the gap.

BLUE CAT   Keep to the right except to pass.

THE BLUE CAT ADDRESSES
HIS GRADUATING CLASS

If these were ordinary times
    I'd say, "Well done!"
    as they say my grandfather said to each son
    when he first solved a quadratic equation,

but a wild, universal lust for power,
    like a rat-borne plague
    spreading death, has subverted my vague,
    sweet, lonely hopes for admiration.

Call the Moon our new America,
     an impenetrable rock
    as dry and treeless as a digital clock
    repeating each night in pious rogation

as it rides through four-dimensional space,
     "What do you want me to make
    of your diminished selves? What classic
    dredge up for your Web Information?"

Leave it? Oh no! Let me tell you *my* vision
     in which you become
    the tigers you dream, and the final sum
    of your shoreside assignments is surfing salvation,

and all your friends are hot, cool, or smart
     feline freethinkers,
    makers and shakers and blue-tattooed tinkers,
    free-loving cats in a cat-loving nation.

SAINTS & TRIPPERS

Look: the blue cat climbs the acid trees
    spaced out between his groovy knees,
        the gray-domed vault of limpid vision,
            the sugared teeth, the lips' collision—
        Peace, brother.

Transparencies: his pearled eye sees
    her yellow hair strung on the breeze
        like smoke, her ears two cloverleaves
            whorled by the cops' sticks then reeved
        in peace, brother.

His stoned mind floats like vegetables
    down the Seine to Notre Dame in the capital
        of the world. His feelings rise like Bach,
            glass notes tumbling out of rock
            (Peace, brother)

from Gabriel's trumpet in spiral love,
    betrayed by what they're not afraid of:
        Death bled red that alkaline cat;
            overhead hangs his cardinal hat:
        Peace, brother.

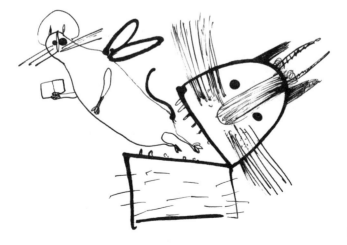

HOME RUN

Exactly i am
traveling i
see
n. y. c.
see
common toms
Grimes
Napoleonic claws
performances
congresses
ceramics

Gristedes
printemps
today.

Of course, Madam,
travel broadens—
a nuclear opportunity.
In Florence
my companion said
and 1,000
mutinied
on the spot.
How many
tonight
are
dead?

The base angles
of isosceles
triangles

are
180
minus what?
The penultimate Mason
is on the verge
of
freezing
loving
?

Bergman
Rohmer
Buñuel
paaaah!

Christmas
Provolone
electric snow
you

asleep
yes, you

knock knock
who's
the curtains
the rugs
the chairs
the beds
are
no
who
yes
dead?
Au printemps
ceramics
philately
spark plugs
yes

i am exactly
see
here.
Come in.

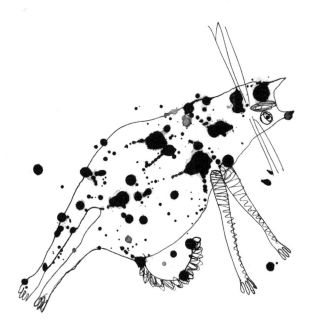

THE BLUE CAT'S DAUGHTER

A girl glides by on rollerblades, her gloves
    waving in the saffron evening air.
    Who wouldn't cut a feather for her hair
swinging like ten pendulums in love?
        Her firefly eyes
        blink through the sky.

What shallop symmetry burst from the hawse
    of her father? Bare-bellied like the moon, she slats
    upon the local all-night lagoon. Cats
at anchor swing to the facts of her windless cause.

The lids of her eyes
batten the sky.

Down, down: Her sultry body dives
like a swan with hands into the terrible dawn.
The water ripples on the standard lawn,
then with the tide backs out of the modern drive.
Her drowned eyes
pull down the sky.

HE FORETELLS HIS PASSING

I can imagine, years from now, your coming back
to this high, old, white house. "Home" I shouldn't say
because we can't predict who'll live here with a different name.
How tall the birches will be then. Will you look up
from the road past the ash for light in the study windows
upstairs and down? Go climb the black maple as first
in new sneakers you walked forty feet in air
and saw the life to come. Don't forget the cats.

Because you grow away from a house, no matter how much you
  come back,
if the people you love are elsewhere, or if the reason is, say,
nostalgia, don't worry about small changes or lost names.
Sit down for a minute under the tallest birch. Look up
at the clouds reflected in the red barn's twisted window.
Lean on the wall. Hear our voices as at first
they shook the plaster, laughed, then burned in the dry air
like a wooden house. I imagine you won't forget the cats.

THE BLUE CAT RUMBLE

Wearing an afro as big as a bush
    the blue cat told me to blow:
"Ain't nothing you can do around here
    'cept pack your ass and go.
    Ain't no business here
    for cats the color of snow."

His mother was a long-haired whore
    who twice a year at least
persuaded half the local boys
    to do the two-backed beast.

Not even a Siamese twist
could make her confess to a priest.

So, who his father is or was
nobody knows or cares.
He snakes his tail around his feet,
his claws cut into the tar;
he sways his head like a tree
and shakes like a stone-filled jar.

"You semitic sham, you shipman's hose,
you moth-eaten fagot of fleas,
I is the word and the light combined.
and I'm getting rid of these.
I'm cleaning out the shits,
like my uncle Hercules."

I shifted right, ready to spring,
my weight on all four paws,
because in matters of peace-or-war

you've got to temper the laws
of thermodynamics and speed
with modifying claws.

I went for his throat; he went for my rump;
I went for his two furred balls.
We spun around in a wailing sound
then fell as an airplane falls
down a manhole into the sewer,
the tubular Underground Halls.

The blue cat raised his hand as a sign
to follow wherever he led.
A beautiful tiger was whoring in back
with dogs on a dirty bed.
A Persian was pulling the hypos
out of its pincushion head.

A hundred kittens were sucking the teats
of a gargantuan leopardess while

forty black panthers paraded the scene
and swept everything out of the aisle.
Before me appeared a fox
in the latest mini style.

A deacon enjoined a prayer for my soul;
the fox gave a flick of her tail.
We fused upon the wastes of Hell
like a solitary sail.
We rounded up the world,
then set it, calm and pale,

in revolutionary motion.
Having changed our planet's
course, we composed a telescopic
verse with which to scan it.
But love outspoken dies:
The selfish readers damned it.

When I awoke the stage was gone,
    the asphalt street was bare.
Vanishing over the rise of the hill
    the blue cat's afro hair
    carried away the hope
    that I could be loved and fair.

"You son of a bitch," I snarled at his back,
    "you ain't changing a thing.
You can stew in the juice of your rotting head
    and suck your tail in a ring.
    I'm the boss of this block for good
    like an old-time English king."

Out of the silence from over the hill
    a haunting laugh replied:
"You mother-fucking, pig-loving cat,
    you're glassy buttons inside.
    You don't mean nothing to me,
    and I got nothing to hide.

Tomorrow night I'm coming up;
    I'll meet you wherever you are.
And when I'm through I'll have you pickled
      and shown in a 2-lb. jar.
      Then the science boys can prove,
      Baby, that's how things are."

What really gets me, I want to say,
    is not the dogs or the laws
or even the different colors of fur,
      but the similar shapes of claws.
      I'd give up this block, I think,
      if there weren't any wars.

COMMUNICATING
WITH THE BEYOND

Green peppers hang from the purple trees,
    from bruised, barren, autumn bones.
This is the orchard of the Pharisees;
    these are the public telephones.
The blue cat waits, still as clay,
    for the decadal, harmonic grace.

There is the cat with the withered hand:
    What does that sheep cry from the pit?
On the olive hills the gored land

bleeds, blind and dumb, but the hypocrite
guards his wheat. *Not you, not here*
    reverberates to the Red Sea.

As bitter as burnt almonds is
    the aftertaste of city love.
Streets divide. The house that was His
    lies empty. In the chill air a dove
calls its mate to the south, prays
    her again to play the queen.

Poetomu ja otrekajus',
    convicted of unworthiness,
self-suspicious, hollow of purpose,
    schooled, like a rabbi, to petty business.
I have been in Hell, have seen
    the black fruit on the black trees.

The tender bodies in Gehenna burn
    like wet leaves. The stillborn air

muffles the farewells. Concerned
     officials kneel in public prayer;
Anathema Maran atha,
     who will get the beekeeper's job?

Pepper seeds drop from dry mouths. Words
     circle the new electric garden.
Out of the current, commanding the herd,
     comes the voice of the dying warden:
Why have you forsaken me?
     The blue cat shrugs and passes on.

Alone, he now lives on the moon,
     in the gaunt bank of our common sorrow.
He stares down the sun each noon
     and sings to stars that may go out tomorrow.
The music we hear in the azure sky
     is the blue cat's orchestra passing by.

THE GOVERNMENT CALLS UPON THE BLUE CAT
TO MAKE A SACRIFICE

*"A study by UNICEF found that [because of depleted uranium] between
1991 and 1998 there were 500,000 deaths above the anticipated rate
among Iraqi children under five. . . . We have to change the United Nations,
to reclaim what is ours. The genocide in Iraq is the test of our will."*

—John Pilger, *The Independent* 23 Feb 03

Remember the tale of the dog, the cat, and the ham?
The old cat scouted the joint; the dog nabbed the meat;
    two bow-legged cheats lying low like shades on the lam,
    the dog kept saying "Our dinner"; the cat, "My ham."
At their hideaway hut the cat raced up a tree

with the meat, polished it off, and called down,
licking his chops, "Friendship demands

    everyone sacrifice something, young man."

"Now what does the world expect," the Blue Cat inquired,
"to compensate for what long ago transpired?

    Not mine my ancestors' greed, nor the dominant view

    that the world will go to the dogs whatever I do.
Trust in heaven? Cut back on catnip and cod?

    Send kittens to war? Pray to a canine god?
I refuse. Henceforth we cats must purge," he said,

    "not the innocent army which the Pied Piper led

    but the rats who betrayed them and left them for

    dead."

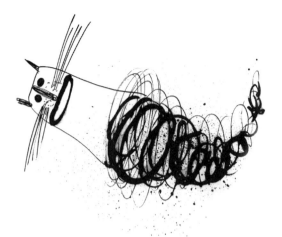

LIVE & LET LIVE: I GOTTA TALK TO YOU

"There is no cure for AIDS."

When I consider how my nights are spent
in blind back alleys where no one gives a damn
who dies and passing *strawberries* raise the rent
on every corner we go *chercher la femme*
(the sport of kings since chorus kittens first
swung their tails), I tell you I resent
love's modern penalties, of which the worst
is the devastating virus monkeys sent

around the world, jealous, like dogs, that cats
always get what they want without tipping their hats.

Who in fact is most affected by bad blood?
You T-cell loser curled up on a heating grate,
you Persian fat cat looking down on urban crud—
rich or poor, *rave no more 'gainst time or fate;*
greed has globalized both bad and good;
you know the longed-for cure will come too late
for us whose bones will sink in Hudson mud
when they fling us out of the way, unable to tolerate
our public dying or *to skin a cat*
to make way for a blueblood commissariat.

No job, no money, no food, no medicine:
Ding dong bell, pussy's in the well—
our poverty's our vice, our sex they call a sin,
they foreclose our mortgages or make us sell;
this is the most savage government that's ever been,
a pack of Cerberuses up from Hell

kicking science out and locking terror in.
Pain to remember, double pain to foretell
the death-in-life that overtakes sick cats
in working-stiff caps or Gucci gloves and spats.

It's true a well-hung tom patrols each street
and nightly sweeps the cuties off their feet,
so what can we do to stop AIDS' fatal spread
but purify love and every cat-lover's bed?
We'll arrange a Platonic symposium on what's
the coolest way to make love—no *ifs, ands* or *buts*—
and strictly enforce the delegates' every motion.
No more pariahs! Long live all loving cats,
male and female bronzed with one tanning lotion!
To the immortality of sex I take off my hat.

THE BLUE CAT PONDERS
HIS SOCIAL POSITION

My uncle was a reprobate;
he ran his father into debt.
One day the poor old man cried out,
"Basta!" and dispatched a note
to the *Inquirer* and the *Telegram*:
"Henceforth Henry's on his own."
Henry loved himself so much
he bought a new ten-gallon hat
             and went west in that.

Of course the family felt disgraced;
my father started his own climb
by moving up to Sutton Place
with thirteen long-haired concubines,
a wet bar and a motorcycle.
The ladies loved his curtain calls;
his cousins envied how he did it;
"When you have a high-point hand," he said,
        "you bid it."

Gambling is a noble vice
among the fashionable set
but intercourse is more than nice
like mountain climbing in Tibet
where one starts higher and gets nearer
to good cigars at the Anglers' Club
and the wives of Wall Street financiers.
Up went my father; down, his brother—
        balanced out each other—

but left their children in a pickle
who didn't know which road to take—
poor and pure (though hair shirts prickle)
or rich and unconscionably fake.
Aphrodite (that was her name)
went on the stage to make some money,
which she did (and a little fame)
until she found for all she won she
> lost the game.

Ares, on the other hand,
stole half of Father's concubines
because he was a gorgeous hunk
and had the family feline spunk.
The ladies went off arm-in-arm
each like a queen that leaves a hive
around whom dizzy workers swarm
to prove that labor keeps one alive:
> Ares praised Allah.

If you ask me I'd say it's moot
what comes from schmoozing with the dealer;
some cats say prayer's the shortest route
to heaven; some sniff it with their feelers;
and some, like me, decide to plow
through the universal give-and-take
because, as every loser knows,
anything but chance is fake—
        fame comes and goes.

A scuttled ship can be refloated,
a dented fender can be repaired,
but a social wreck is not a boat or
vehicle for a *Vanity Fair*.
Education's the way to go
(as democratic a way as any);
and so I went up block by block
from Castle Garden to Harlem Meer
with mastery of slang and sneer
and bib and tucker and clean white socks
        like a millionaire.

Crowned with success and a new top hat,
I dashed around like electricity;
I promised citizens felicity—
I reserved nine lives for every cat—
I waited for revenge to come,
for who turned Dick Whitington back toward London
then set bells ringing? It was I.
And who in a zigzag led Dante
              up Mount Paradise?

A cat can go without a shot
at love, his confidence's so great,
but not without the rich romances
of the night. I think of Uncle Henry
doomed to an impecunious state
for having forsworn the sweet nuances
of the dark, and how my old man ended
with having less than he pretended;
              I hate Fate.

When the dove comes fluttering toward me low
and vexed (O jealousy, not justice)
I'll scratch out its two pink eyes to show
that still the Furies punish hubris.
The kleptocrats whose knives and guns
keep things unequal have never won
my love; their endless wars are Hell.
　　No cat boarded Old Noah's Ark.
　　We and the Moon still run the dark
　　　where we cast our spells.

HE CONTEMPLATES SEX

October is the sweetest month
        when summer's foison fills the air
with promises of fall accounting
        and a sultry Persian's silky hair
to curl up in against the weather:
        a courtesan, a sunlit square—
        dorade for supper and a pair
        of tickets to *Yarochintsy Fair*—
        O for the life of the debonair!

A cat that has unrivalled prowess
　　　　　escorts a film star to the Met
on opening night and afterwards
　　　　　embraces the singers on the set,
drives his girls about top down,
　　　　　refuses to be a parlor pet,
　　　　　makes sure no fish falls from his net,
　　　　　blow-dries his head when it gets wet,
　　　　　and keeps a yacht with a bi-valet.

Lovemaking isn't for the faint-hearted:
　　　　　to bed a tantrum-throwing Siamese
demands an eremitic concentration,
　　　　　and he who thinks he knows how to please
a streetwise tabby has forgot
　　　　　she can bounce an army on her knees;
　　　　　love's perfume rides the evening breeze
　　　　　but canters off at a vulgar sneeze,
　　　　　or gets blown away like autumn leaves.

No point in yin/yang calculation:
>   there's always someone better off
and someone worse— O king of cats
>   in Africa, *ave! mazel tov!*
But sugarplum, Far Eastern sister,
>   blue-tipped, brown-furred, sloe-eyed, soft
>   and silky Lady Smerdiakov,
>   let's buzz on down to my Soho loft
>   where time perfects what haste pulls off.

THE BLUE CAT LEADS A PROTEST

One day this cat comes into the bar,
    head big as a melon, jaws ajar,
leans on an elbow and orders a beer
    like any one of the regulars here,
        like one of the regulars here.

You could see by his paws and the cut of his cap
    that he was an old-fashioned longshoring cat;
with the hook in his belt and the brogue on his tongue
    he could part the waters like Moses done,
        lead his people like Moses done.

It was Ralph who rose to the challenge to say
    "I ain't never seen you before this way;"
the cat replied that probably was
    on account of Ralph's being one of the fuzz,
      for being one of the fuzz.

That riled the boys, who circled round,
    ready to flatten him to the ground,
but he downed his beer and leapt on the bar
    knocking over the peanut jar,
      knocking over the jar.

"Boys," he said, "I'll tell you the truth,
    a working man's life goes with his youth;
the day he turns fifty and his pension comes up
    they drop him like lead and he gets a tin cup,
      he's left holding out a tin cup.

The older you get the less you can do,
    so they're installing computers in place of you

on the assembly line, and whatever they can
    they manufacture in Yucatán,
        they outsource to Yucatán.

Steel mills are closing; planes fall from the sky—
    Work is respected? In a pig's eye!
You stand with each other but who gets the cash?
    And who hits the ground when the scaffoldings crash?
        Who goes down when the scaffoldings crash?"

As he grew more inspired he hiked up his pants
    and started doing a gandy dance,
a hornpipe of sorts like he was a tar
    in New York City in a working-class bar,
        in a New York working-class bar.

"Some's yellow," he says; "some's black or ecru;
    some's red, some's white—take me, I'm blue—
but the world out that door don't see us the same,
    'cause keeping us separate's the name of the game—
        goin' to change the name of the game."

"Follow me!" he cried with a seven-league leap
　　　to the chandelier and then to the street
where he launched a parade like the Pied Piper once,
　　　only he promised to come back for lunch,
　　　　　he swore they'd be back for lunch.

One thousand joined his conga line,
　　　then two, then ten, a million prime—
not counting women and children—men,
　　　all on a march for work again,
　　　　　marching to work again.

The deputy mayor comes out of town hall,
　　　then the whole city council, liars and all;
the mayor addressed them from the top of the steps,
　　　and even the governor sent down his reps,
　　　　　the governor called on his reps.

Two hours haranguing with "this" and then "that,"
　　　none of which moved the republican cat,
who brought up the subject of social change

as the mounted police rode into range,
    as the mounties rode into range.

The fight that ensued left ten thousand dead—
    not counting the women, the kids, and the Reds.
They swept up the bodies from Chamber to John
    and stashed them away in Turtle Pond,
      dumped all of them into the pond.

Of course the cat never showed for lunch,
    but a cat like that has nine lives: I've a hunch
(his remains have never been found) like the rest
    he got laid off doing what he did best,
      he vanished doing his best.

I'm glad you stopped in to ask if I
    or anyone here wants pie in the sky;
we're proud to do the work we do
    but tired of being economically screwed,
      tired of being screwed.

Some say there'll be a Second Coming
      when all the factories again will start humming,
but I don't know. What do *you* think?
      Meanwhile, what would you like to drink?
        Tell me, what do you drink?

The following pictures were taken by Sean Sime at the premiere of *The Return of the Blue Cat* at the Harold Clurman Center for Poetry, Christopher Goodrich director, of the Stella Adler Studio in New York City on March 29th, 2004. Sonny Paladino is the pianist; Mike Buchwald, the drummer; Ed Griffin, the bass player.

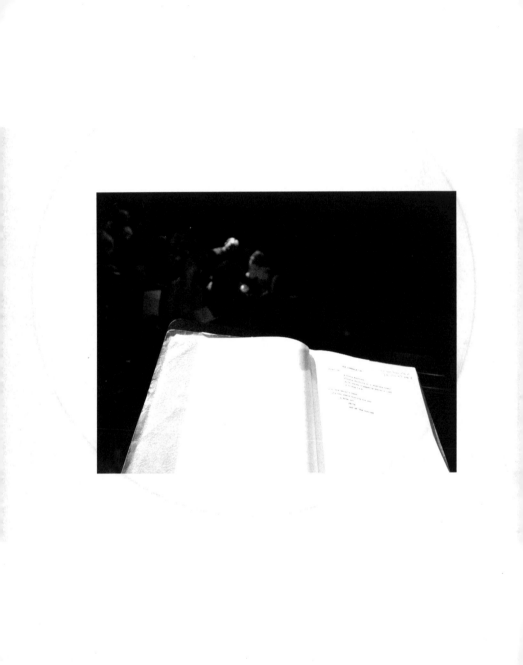

THE RETURN OF THE BLUE CAT
F. D. Reeve and Exit 59

CD playlist

1. The Comeback Cat
2. The Blue Cat at the Laundromat
3. Identity Crisis
4. The Blue Cat Studies History's Lessons, Part I
5. The Blue Cat Studies History's Lessons, Part II
6. Early Morning in White River Junction
7. The Blue Cat & the Parrot
8. The Blue Cat Addresses His Graduating Class
9. Saints & Trippers
10. Home Run
11. The Blue Cat's Daughter
12. He Foretells His Passing
13. The Blue Cat Rumble
14. Communicating with the Beyond
15. The Government Calls upon the Blue Cat to Make a Sacrifice
16. Live & Let Live: I Gotta Talk to You
17. The Blue Cat Ponders His Social Position
18. He Contemplates Sex
19. The Blue Cat Leads a Protest

The author and musicians would like to express their gratitude to the Northern Track Recording Studio and Gary Henry, engineer and Colby Dix, mix engineer.